Essential Question
What is a folktale?

The Magic Paintbrush

retold by Amy Helfer

illustrated by Ethan Long

PAIRED READ Poetry/Song: **Wanted: A Friend . . 13**

Once upon a time, there was a girl named Lin-Lin. She wanted a paintbrush.

One day, Lin-Lin wakes up.
She sees a paintbrush
on her bed.

She says, "Is it a magic
paintbrush?"

bed

Lin-Lin paints an orange.
The orange becomes real!

The paintbrush can make
pictures real!

People come from far away.
They ask Lin-Lin for help.
Lin-Lin paints what they need.

A man named Chang takes the paintbrush.

He says, "I will be rich and happy!"

First, Chang paints a robe.
Then he paints gold.
Both things become real.

But Chang is not happy.

He says, "I want to swim."

Chang takes the gold
with him. Then he walks
to the sea.

sea

Chang can not swim. The gold is so heavy!

Lin-Lin asks a man in a boat to help.

Chang says, "Take your
paintbrush, Lin-Lin. I don't
need any gold. I just need
a friend like you."

Respond to Reading

Retell

Use your own words to retell *The Magic Paintbrush*.

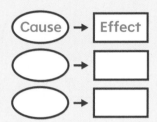

Text Evidence

1. Look at page 5. Why do people ask Lin-Lin for help?

   Cause and Effect

2. Look at page 10. Why can't Chang swim? Cause and Effect

3. How do you know that *The Magic Paintbrush* is a folktale?

   Genre

Compare Texts
Read about making new friends.

Wanted: A Friend

by Julia Jakes

I want a friend.
How can I get one?
I ask my mom.
She says I must be one.

Dad tells me this,
"It's not a race."
Next Grandma says,
"Put a smile on your face."

Just be myself
Is what I will do.
And soon I will have
a friend or two!

Make Connections

What did Chang learn about friends? What did the child in the poem learn? **Text to Text**

Focus on  Genre

Folktale A folktale is a story based on traditions. A folktale often teaches a lesson. The events in the story are not real.

What to Look for In *The Magic Paintbrush,* Chang learns that friends are more important than gold. This is a lesson. The paintbrush is magic. Paintbrushes are not magic in real life.

Your Turn

Think about the lesson that Chang learns in this story. Draw a picture that shows what he learns. Share your picture with the class.